Ways of Light

Ways of Light.

Poems 1972-1980

RICHARD EBERHART

NEW YORK   OXFORD

OXFORD UNIVERSITY PRESS

1980

Copyright © 1980 by Richard Eberhart

Library of Congress Cataloging in Publication Data
Eberhart, Richard, 1904-
Ways of light.
I   Title
PS3509.B456W38   811'.5'2   79-25150
ISBN 0-19-502737-X

Printed in the United States of America

Ways of Light.

Poems 1972-1980

RICHARD EBERHART

NEW YORK   OXFORD
OXFORD UNIVERSITY PRESS
1980

Copyright © 1980 by Richard Eberhart

Library of Congress Cataloging in Publication Data
Eberhart, Richard, 1904-
Ways of light.
I   Title
PS3509.B456W38   811'.5'2   79-25150
ISBN 0-19-502737-X

Printed in the United States of America

To

My wife
My children
And grandchildren

To

My wife
My children
And grandchildren

Acknowledgments

I am grateful to the Editors of the following publications
in which some of the poems in this book first appeared:

American Poetry Review   The Atlantic Monthly
The Berkeley Review   Chicago Review
Friends of the Smith College Library   Guide to the Arts
The Harvard Advocate   *Into the Round Air*   A Local Muse
London Times Literary Supplement
New England Review   New Statesman   *The Poetry Anthology*
Poetry   The New York Quarterly   *Two Poems*   The Tower
The Virginia Quarterly Review   *Survivors*, Boa Editions (1979).
   "Under the Hill" first appeared in *Poetry* in 1927.

Contents

Those ways of light
Which who in death would live to see
Must learn in life to die like thee.

A Hymn to the Name and Honor
of the Admirable Saint Theresa

RICHARD CRASHAW (1613-1649)

Rifkin Movement

Don't let it mean anything,
Hold back the meaning,
But let it flow.

Sweet, strong, and pure,
Your piano is your soul,
Let it flow.

Let America go,
Let it struggle with its fate, but
Let it flow.

A quiet voice is beneficent,
No bombs, no assassinations,
Let it flow.

Let it flow, Rifkin,
Let it flow,
Your piano, noble, American.

Let it flow, Joplin,
From your grave,
Give me your song
Day long.

Under the Hill

When darkness crept and grew
The hushed wide earth lay still.
I listened; I thought I knew
The vibrance under the hill.
If I were now just dead
I could not make less sound.
I slowly bent my head
Intently to the ground.
I listened again. My feet
Took root within the soil;
Earth grew within me, sweet
In my limbs. I knew the soil
Had claimed my body whole.
I listened. There came no sound
Across the darkening knoll
Or over the matted ground.

I had become a thing
Of earth. My face felt air
As leaves feel winds that bring
A sudden cool. My hair
Was grass, my flesh was sand—
Strange that it happened there
Upon the solid land!
My blood turned water. My bone
Took on the strength of stone.
Mixed with earth and sky,
I bore all things to die.

I caused the twig to sprout
And every flower come out.
Flaming the earth with spring
I made each robin sing,
Then sent the long heat down
Tinging green leaves with brown.
I made the summer old
With singing autumn gold,
And stilled all things that grow,
And covered the world with snow.

When darkness crept and grew
The hushed wide earth lay still.
Being earth, at last I knew
The vibrance under the hill.

Angels and Man

What stirs imagination is the impossibility
Of honesty because of complexity,
You would think there was an honesty
And that it would be as simple as truth,
The truth you knew as a child
When everything was immediate and real
And the truth was what you saw and felt
And these were in a miracle of unison
Which only seemed a miracle many lives later
When diversity, change, and disunity
Corroded the spirit to endless diversity
But then truth was final, powerful, and absolute.
You had an absolute hold on nature and love,
Your energies were boundless and man no enemy,
You walked in nature as one in rapture,
The vocabulary of explicit dictionaries
Could not match the wordless passion
Into which you walked with occult delight,
And there could not be sufficient definition
For the endless joy you felt in existence.

It was in the jungle among the brambles and vines
You knew the precise movement of small animals,
In this thicket your body and mind in harmony
Knew what it was to be alive, to rejoice,
To sense danger, and to be immediate master of fear,
And you knew an ecstasy at the heart of poetry.
Moving to the garden, leaving aboriginal wildness,

You saw the ordered rows of the planted vegetables
And so fell in love with the glory of lettuces
That you saw angels atop the lettuce plants,
A vision so pure it would strike your frame for decades,
And when heavy realities drained the passionate youth
You would think of the taking away of the angels
As some mystery too deep to comprehend,
For they were gone, the garden of the world destroyed,
But you had seen the angels atop the lettuce plants
With reality and finality of inevitable love.

Out of the extraordinary thicket into
The planted garden, from wilderness to order.
What was the new adventure of the strangeness of life?
It was the orchard. For here in the orchard
A new richness appeared in the neon spectacle
Of acres of apple blossoms ladening air with scent
In a largess hard to believe. I walked enchanted
In the height of May in a sensory exultance
As if life had given me a promise too rich to keep
But it was only months later that I realized
The excellence of sumptuousness, sensual gain
When the red apples bent down the heavy boughs
And we bore the red apples to the cider mill,
Although they were already an ancient symbol
Of man's fall by the temptress Eve,
And then, O then, I shall keep the scent
Welling up from the juices of the fruit
Loved as if one, bound in Attica,
Appropriated the greatness of life.

To be honest is to find fault
With the lying and the cheating years,
The many years, the deaths, the destructions
Which take away the messages of truth
You knew when you were young
And bring in their stead no resolutions,
No finality as real as the thicket,
The garden and the orchard, no sense of truth,
But ever the deeper problem of mature man
Whose intellect would raise some kind of absolute
But whose heart spends itself in a wilderness
Without assurance, as he knows too much
And feels too little, and cannot regain
The stupendous vision life gave him in the beginning,
Which time takes away from him toward his end.

I salute the spirit of life, and I rejoice
In one glimpse of timeless truth,
The wildness of the thicket, the order of the garden,
And the apples, O the red apples of the orchard,
Symbol of the rich heart, the unresolved enigmas of man.
The intellect violates the vision of youth.
It shakes reality, but it is not true.
What is the truth? One was only
A young live animal in the jungle,
Expressing life. The angels atop
The lettuce leaves have left me ever since.
They torment me with their beauty
But they do not exist, they vanished,
Only real in contemplation and memory.
The garden, a prime symbol of the world,
Is yet great and unattainable,

The orchard, something given of richness,
Sensual, a perfume of apples and blood,
Non-metaphysical, the baseness of our nature,
Sumptuousness of the actual and the real,
Dissatisfied me at the base of my nature
Because sucking life I demanded to suck on death.
Nature did not have enough in it of philosophy.
In the midst of life in imbibing apple cider
I realized I was one who was enchanted,
I was held in the enchantment of the world,
In the heart of delight I knew despair
For the rich orchard had not divorced me from time.
Even as I drank with gusto the cider
I knew that I would not be alive for long
And dreamed of centuries beyond the span of life.

We are too impatient to wait for answers,
Waving our arms about in wildness,
As I saw those of my grandfather waving
When I was tender and young, he in his eighties,
Itinerant preacher, and his hands flailed
The air as if expecting an overwhelming question,
I felt, through him, historical richness.
And my mother, soon to die, tried to
Lift the tall old man into his bed
As I took my first knowledge of death.
Now fifty years later I sense
My arms flailing at ultimate questions,
Unanswered, the questions of man.

In the Air

There is something more than meets the eye.
It is a sky
Of ineffable richness.

It is as if the senses
Knew truth,
But knew it was a lie.

The senses in their swirl
Of immediacy
Feel something beyond.

Women in their love
Know never,
Guess Cleopatra, Heloise.

Men in ambition,
Fired and high,
Think of Apollo, Dionysus.

There is something more than meets the eye,
A rustle in the leaves
Suggests Daphne unperceived.

It is a sky so high
Nothing in it will die,
Or be fully known.

A great essence,
The sensorium
Of ineluctability.

A magical element,
Supremest insight,
Just felt.

Every day
Takes it away
Brings it again.

There is something more than meets the eye,
Spring and Fall,
That I recall.

Interior Winter Sequence

All the deaths make love more valuable.

Richer than the past, the present
Brings gentleness and silence,
New integers
In a world of brutality and noise,

Gentleness, comes gentleness,
Arms' caresses better than arms that fight,
A reality deeper than speech,
To which speech is an approximation,

Riches of decades in a single hour,
Concentrate of freedom, complete,
Concretion of invisibles,
The senses able to withstand the senses,

All the subtleties of relationships
Forgotten and remembered,
Remembered and forgotten,
As peace falls into its place.

All the lives make love more valuable.

It is a sequence of variables
Seeming to be inviolable,
The imagined unreality reality,
Senses expert beyond sensation,

Yet nothing absolute articulated,
Nothing not human premeditated,
Anything is as possible as freedom,
The cat sleeps on the bed, unphilosophic.

If words could be as delicate as touch
They would write themselves into nighttime
As nothing but the everything they can say
About joy without overcoming joy.

Words must be erect, tensile, strong
To put into the realm of reality
Unreality, invisibilities, subtleties
That ravish the senses and the mind.

Los Arcos
La Paz

The dogs are barking
The cocks are crowing
All night, all night

And in the brightest light
Of brightest day
In pristine La Paz,

The big black buzzards
Sleek and huge, in droves
Wheel and light on the fronds.

They are just above our heads,
Cleanest black on cleanest green,
Seen from a little pool.

How they wheel, the big birds
While down the beach, strewn with shells
Some miles of Southern silence

In loneliest Pacific reaches
High, almost out of sight, the albatross!
What resolution, what direction!

A pelican plays nearby, playfellow
Pelican as the fish jump where green
Water turns to blue. We wade.

On the hill back in the town,
Incredibly clear, the orphans chant,
Paced by a solicitous nun.

The big peninsula that ends in an arch
In bluest blue of the white-sanded Pacific
Proffers papaya, salt-encrusted Margueritas

While the sumptuous black birds
Wheel overhead, light in the palm fronds.
In a bright hot Mexican glow

We ride days of idleness,
Mariachi players on the porch at dusk,
A man sings softly through the dawn.

Love Sequence with Variations

I

There ought to be some sign of Spring.
We cannot endure the coldness, the harshness.
Could we have evolved a feeling for Spring
If we were fated to blindness in a Winter cave?

There ought to be some sign of Spring.
The only good thing about harsh Winter
Is to make love in the dark, as the snows fall.
That is to take the hell out of darkness.

We instinctively know each day will be longer.
The god of youth will come over the world,
There will be buds, fine days, and then flowers,
But light! light! light! praise to light!

One look of climax in a girl's face
Brings a sense of ecstasy and glory.
Springtime, love light of evanescence,
This is to put the heaven into life.

II

Love is magical, improbable, a god
Remarkable and holy that lights on mortals.
Exult at the exaltation of this state,
Unpredictable, given to changing the world.
It is shy at first, remarkably persistent,
The young are in the toils of ancient strength,
Why has it not happened to these two before?
It is the mystical bond of physical touch.
They touch, they feel, their eyes bound on one double string,
A new day has begun among our friends
Astounded at a change so great in a time so short,
Love is magical, illogical, and true.
Why of all people in the world
Have you chosen me, why have I chosen you?

III

When talking of love one cannot easily avoid
The lecturer's stance: we have seen lovers cool,
Congeal, fracture, shatter to fragments of personality,
The god having gone out of them to the skies,
Leaving them lowly and surly in despair,
Or leaving them more or less as they were,
But scarred and maimed from so high a flight,
Now suffering from being themselves and low.

The lecturer tends to take the comic stance
Seeing that men and women, intelligent and eye-worthy,
Called into passion by the god of love,
Are so complex, so conditioned by the past,
That often they cannot keep it up,
Relationship becomes a long contest of wills,

And if there are children the children suffer,
Although divorce is now so common among us
That they have to redefine the idea of mother
And father, swim in the tides as they are able.
Men and women go from one to another,
Or live alone, or go for each other, or sometimes
Draw the gun, or put their head in the oven,
From the horror of life and the boredom of the soul.

Too much intellect may be a bane
Drawing lovers apart by overweening argument,
Just as stupidity, not perceived in love's blindness,
May become an equal and wrecking torture,
And indeed the lecturer on the life of love
Reading a thousand specialists, guffaws.

For so intricate are the problems, the advents
Of sexual freedom and repression, the ills
Of loving or lack of loving or partial loving,
Or the aftermaths of wholly passionate loving,
Or wholly permissive loving, that bewilderment
Often overcomes, as it sometimes overwhelms,
The protagonists of a changing democracy,
Where every idea is challenged, and nothing is ideal.

Love cannot be divorced from money, the lecturer
Says, but if money could be divorced from lovers
It might put them back in a state of nature,
Envying Rousseau, and let them till the land,
Drink fresh air, and live on vegetables.
This might be a vigorous reincarnation of the real.

IV

Nobody else knows your secret love,
Nobody else can know your secret love
So that the new relation of a face,
Magically meshing into other imaged faces,
Banned from consciousness to the mysterious
Totality of ecstatic joy which wordless, instant,
Is also subliminal ecstasy of renowned sorrow,
And all in a dreaming time of great richness,

This state is so baffling, baffled in Paradise,
One is extended to the reaches of the being,
Confused, ununderstanding, totally seized and struck
With the remarkable reorganization of love's excellence,
Past faces with a new face intertwined
Beyond reason, in blurred sweetness of infinity.

It is a magical state where the world offers,
Haphazard, a new evidence of the possible,
Unexpected presentation of love instantly known,
So overpowering as to benumb the senses,
Which, in their rich confusion, cannot separate out
One face from many faces back to youth,
To the mother of all eventualities,
One cannot know which face is mastering

But stunned as if by a vision of angels,
In such a delight as to be beyond action,
Delight in color and line, subjective power
Radiating out and changing the universe,
It is an experience and totality of bliss
As when love's arrow pierced the breast of St. Theresa.

V

Love is the autonomy of the soul
Seeking disjunction; this disjunctive force,
Running along the skin like a cruel snake,
Presses the soul to a strange enticement,
Saying to get with the world as it is,
This drama is known to every man and woman,
Ancient as the first thinker, who thought to be
Alone, draw ideal pictures on the cave wall.

But then we see Laocoon the strong man,
Writhing in the toils of writhing snakes,
Caught in the coils and recoils of reality,
Anguish on his visage, weakness in his arms,
And we never thought that this horrible vision
Would be the savage truth of the world, and ours.

But when we sought to release and lose
The autonomy of the soul, in a disjunctive release
That would give a glad hand to possibility,
Invite the world to reach out with peace and plenty,
When we put out tendril vines of aspiring love,
The green time, the high hope, songs of belief,
Fervent, active, urgent, passionate, carefree,
In luminous rites of levitating harmonies,

We were forced back by awful recognition,
And no man has a soul strong enough
To withstand the blows of fate, deadly strokes
Aimed at the heart of our innocent care,
And as years beat down every man to the ground,
He calls his soul back to the silence of prayer.

But prayer will not help, and man is alone,
And out in the wide world where murder is daily,
In the streets where whites shoot blacks, blacks shoot whites,
In the cities, accomplishers of every evil,
In far places where mighty, gun-blue nations
Rain bombs on small victims without
A twinge of conscience, or the slightest ability
To love anybody else as they love themselves,

The thinking man, the man of feeling, alone
With a sense of kindness, love, and justice,
Is hard put to it to make sense of existence,
As if all the wisdom of the world were nothing,
The mystical beliefs of every major religion,
Destroyed by barbarians, the barbarous heart.

VI *Making Love to a Page*

I approach this page with insolence and reverence
For I would break out of myself and love another.
It is not a page in velvet in the court of Elizabeth,
It is not a page of Sir Walter Raleigh,
It is not the rough youth who proffered the hard cup
To Beowulf, nor one who mocked the thirst of Jesus.
I would make love to the immaculate, the austere pages
On which were written the great poems of the world.

Here I give accord and announce a still reverence
For the purity of every antique papermaker,
The makers of papyri, who made the ground of being,
And for every hand that had a hand in prebirth,
For these men of wonder and of care, in every century,
Were the unacknowledged lovers of poetic genius.

VII

How could I write a poem that would touch
The peculiar wellspring of tears throat-deep
To express careful joy of innocent papermakers
Who did not know that they preserved the heart of Langland,
Cantering Chaucer, changeable Shakespeare, those men
Who made it possible for Pope to indite,

Magical vellums, rags and silks, watery loves.
Who could imagine a praise high enough
For the pages on which Dante wrote his *Commedia,*
The reality of Angelus Silesius, the markings of Beddoes,
Clare writing "Badger," Smart loving his cat Jeoffry,
Who can love enough a page of Keats?

VIII

But of Hopkins the sufferer I write further
And think of his manuscripts, precise, intent,
Who died unknown at the age of forty-four,
As the scandal of genius, the secret heart of man,
For this man, lost before reality's hardship,
Buckled before his ability, and gave us his poems

Shining in reality like the life of his Master,
Peculiar, odd, differing, lovely and enlivening,
And there is no madness, despite Plato,
So rewarding as a true originality of nature
Perceiving subtleties, central truths of nature,
And there is no poet today so exacting as Hopkins.

IX

She glided into his presence like a spirit,
Thin, out of thin air, suddenly was there,
Pervasive insinuation and tactile arrangement,
Moving effortlessly, gazing non-saying.

The gratuity of the occasion peaked astonishment,
Expressive of unexpected newness in the world,
A newness of a delicacy of Shelley
Her extreme fragility yet pervasive strength.

She must have had the mark of the Shelleyan,
Musk of the leopard, flash of the cheetah,
But was all gauze and see-through airiness,
She expanded and diffused herself like a perfume.

A monumental mountainous mentality
Felt a warm soft air from the sea coast,
A wafting toward it of gentle fragrances
Held in a balance of awarenesses.

Then they sank into profound non-being,
Beyond the flesh and beyond the mind,
Which has no metaphor; a reality   .
Out of the world, alone and one.

X

Love is the abstractest singing thing
Its song springing, ever on the wing,
Out of the reach of the flesh which follows
As only its high self it allows.

Love is up there somewhere in the air
Refusing to be caught in bed, or to bear
To be bare, but instead, in the flesh's
Plight, the soul, ravished in its meshes,

Steals away from the body's enjoyment
And nobody knows quite where it went.
The body's completest clutch, the union,
Is limited to a bodily communion

While the soul, the soul of love, superior,
Tells all lovers that they are inferior,
And from somewhere, some great where, up in the air
Gives abstract knowledge to a loving pair.

O believe the flesh is best, in secret,
Love will fly away, be a white egret,
Or dream in the night some Helen come
War comes upon man, strike you down dumb.

Stopping a Kaleidoscope

The world is kaleidoscopic, ever changing,
Pieces falling into place momentarily
To give and fix a world of lights and colors.

Each stop is a strange new situation,
Each decade has its colors and its lights,
Each stop shows the world newly formed.

Abstract yet real, visual excitement,
The kaleidoscope shows, fixes truth without error,
So it seems, fresh views to the young, to the old.

The imagination to toy with this toy
Thinks no stop or view stays permanent,
Has to believe permanence of impermanence.

Eye and hand are too restless not to move it,
A slight or large movement resets bright scenes,
As time has been remaking the world to our view.

Decades shift and fall into place again,
Energies of the world are stable unstable,
Our senses camber the kaleidoscope.

I stop it, and there I see the world of the present,
Manifold reality fixed in a moment of time.
I turn it. It will be the twenty-first century.

Sameness ever the same, ever changing,
Growth and stasis in a hale bemusement,
We know what we see, see what we know.

No ebb, no flow not subject to change,
No changelessness in our consciousness
Remaining, nothing but what Heraclitus told.

Then and Now

What will it all be like
A thousand years from now?
In our passionate excess
We are limited to the now.

Who could see the pterodactyl
Sumptuous in his flight
Battening on the earth,
Efficient day and night?

Who could sense brontosaurus
Mucking through the muck
A huge vegetarian
Munching delicate vegetables?

They died out finally
Because they lacked brains
To change their life styles
Before too much drought, or rains.

Who could see *Homo sapiens*
Putting up the stones of Chartres,
Sounding Beethoven, writing Keats,
Overpopulating the earth?

Now that we have passed him,
He had too many brains,
An animal who could think to think,
Died because he was inane.

Winter Squirrels
in Pine Trees

Two grays looking hale
Out of an upper-story window
Caper on branches munching sprouts,

Happy in their orbit habitat.
They do not have to go far away,
Seem satisfied with where they are.

On the moon two astronauts
In white, with comic dancing motion,
Scrape up some rocks, some dust,

Lose a fender bouncing to the lem,
Want to ask questions of space,
Other creatures, other mechanisms.

The squirrels, aesthetically free,
Astronauts, constrained, awkward.
Mother computer, we are small, bring us in.

Blue Spring

Across the greensward beside the spring
Dancers, men and women, gave their gifts,
Tip-tilted movements in the afternoon,
Vigorous, youthful, precise, in twos or fours,

Or sixes, dancing for discovery, joyful,
Tireless, redemptive, delicately expressive
Beside the blue spring of idea's youth
Flashing our senses with emblems of release.

And as they retire before our blue, yellow,
Green eyes, to partake of wine and food,
A single man, dressed in a loin cloth,
Seen from one side as a Pan, without hooves,

Plays his pipe, a solitary commander
Of the air and time, he orders life and time
With the fingers of an ancient Greek
As he pervades the entered air with airs

Magical and sweet, in the extravagant scene
Of classical perfection in a mortal state,
An afternoon for a surprising fete.
As we leave the spring seems more innately blue.

We swam in amnion, partakers in
Enchantment of the unreal in the real
When color, line, movement, springtime air
Possessed us, and opened up into the new.

The Rose

A blemish appeared upon the petals
Slowly, at first imperceptibly,
I thought that I could brush it away
But soon it was there to stay,

Part of the rose itself.
Of divestiture
I had no power,
In the inhaling hour

Felt the nature of reality,
The rose that seemed perfect
Became like my being
Even while seeing.

I had to reinvest the world,
Clothe it with linens,
Had to destroy grief
To resurrect belief.

Time's Clickings

If the moment could be brought back,
    Clicks through the trees
    The typewriter speaking

        Those summer days of blue-green silence
        Struck by the little bells

And the pleasure of the solitude of the trees,
    Thinking through the days
    The struck delicate messages

        In the time of thoughttransferences
        When shadow was sun, sun was shadow,

The eleemosynary appearance of endlessness
    The surround of wood and water
    of birds flying and breeze passing

        By the pool and the statues and the urn
        Wood-toned smoke, haze off the hayfields

There in the time that was whole and hardy
    While dreams were infallible indices
    of further dreams of dreams

        In the shimmer of noon   the serving
        of summer   in lightest afternoon

If the moment could be brought back
    It would be the truth
    Of the artist writing history

        But he is dead, it is late, and I write
        Memory of Williams writing *Paterson*.

Nostalgia for Edith Sitwell

I wish it were the nineteen-fifties
And I was going to see Dame Edith Sitwell
And Sir Osbert in a restaurant in Boston,
And my friends would be there, and they

Would be sharp and handsome, friendly,
And we would think that the world was great,
And they would think they had a handle on it,
And I would think everything in the world is important

And Edith and Osbert were splendid and imperious
And somehow Death had not taken over the world
So we could be full of grace, with a sense of grandeur,
And O what deep realizations we had of life!

And after the shrimps and the wine and the haleness
We walked onto the streets of present Boston.
Osbert bowed to Dr. Parkinson, and bumped a tree.
He could not stop, so we had to stop him.

We lived when words were like roses on bayonets
With long-nosed Edith, and long-boned Osbert,
Alive to intelligence and to poetry,
Over their shoulders shadows of the Plantagenets.

Word-Prowess

Words were the animals behind the trees,
Amorphous shapes, undefined, which could kill.
Shadowy beasts of prey. We stand them off with skill.
Lovers hear them as easement, as they take their ease.

A man leaped into the pit of a great cat,
Making a preposterous gesture of defiance.
The captive tiger felt the élan of the sense,
Scraped his flesh almost to death at that.

The keeper shot the beast between the eyes.
It was senseless. The man was dragged away
To think about his act another day.
The skies were indifferent, indifferent skies.

Dead beast, futile man. Nature is great,
Words-long. Onto lovers leaps fate.

Robert's Rules of Order

When I was president of Duodecim
There used to be a complicated maneuver
Wherein we went into the committee of the whole.
Whenever we could not decide,
Something had to be deified,
So we obscured our body to make plain our soul.

As one to preside, who had the voice of twelve,
It was my pleasure to make fine distinctions.
Certainly the truth was as a fiery coal.
When our body was at fever heat
Our intelligences thrashed to defeat,
And then we went into the committee of the whole.

Robert's Rules of Order saved our clan.
It brought order out of chaos to a man.
None finally doubted this authority.
We had a final goal
In a kind of over-soul
When we went into the committee of the whole.

I used to know that small red book by heart.
It was my savior through polemic art.
We wanted to be saved by rules of order.
From the abstract, the ultimate distinction,
None could subtract even truth's intinction,
As we found our solution in the committee of the whole.

Opposition

Wildness of nature is in Florida,
Where senses open to the enveloping heat,
Where no Puritan lives, persons respond to excess,
The lust of the idea of Paradise.
Where Ichetucknee springs from limestone depths
Changeless through clear centuries,
As we float tubing down the enchanting stream.

Tameness of nature holds back the North,
Desolations of the past eroding the present,
The long, heavy shadow of the Puritans
Teaches the severe. They thought life could be better,
Prayed to God not to do anything wrong,
Held back their passion, aimed to kill,
Burned as witches free life-loving girls.

Ichetucknee

It is the continuous welling up from the earth
We must remember. Dawn comes, and the waters
Spring fresh, clear, vital from the earth.
Night comes, they well unabated from the dark.

Strange, is it not, that the temperature
Is always the same. The clarity is without change.
As the water blooms upward to become a petaled river
Each grain of sand below is visible as in air.

Over the oval, the mouth, the maw, the source,
We cannot see down into the cavernous mystery
Into primitive limestone releasing the clear water.
We are impelled outward from the warm, strong center.

Our bodies delight in the flow of original life.

Freely in the stream of exhilarating non-history
We can walk, swim, float in the clearest shallows.
Upon us the welling up of the source,
Around us the gift of the river, the way we must go.

Our bodies delight in the flow of original life.

Fat Spider

Thrills, the fat spider
Who comes only in September,
What was she doing in July,

While swallows were nesting
Above a lightbulb in our areaway,
Produced their chicks, who flew away.

While people were coming and going,
Sailors sailing,
Poets making poems,

What was the fat spider doing
Who came out only in September,
As she had each year and years ago?

The fat spider, intelligent,
As nature, wordless, impinges,
Knew when to appear,

Appeared outside my study window,
Twenty paces from the ocean,
To astonish me to her acceptance,

She took glory in existence
Constructing her web in iridescence
As a map of the universe.

Rain came down over the roof
But she had calculated nicely
To spin between the roof and the window.

There the fat spider, queenly,
Ordered her natural existence,
Big and dangerous, fat and sleek,

And caught me off my thinking base,
Because she was so inevitably clean
She would kill everything within reach.

Gnats

A society of gnats
Hangs on a beam of light
Near the ground, toward evening.

Then they rise up
And hang in the air,
Animatedly bunched.

What is their meaning?
I cannot guess their meaning
They are so ephemeral.

Nature makes them come and go,
As it does us. We
Amass our own society,

And I cannot guess our meaning,
Although I have tried for fifty years,
Twisting and turning.

Quarry-Stone

A square of marble
Atop a cut-off pine stump
Looks like winter.

It does not people air,
It is abstract,
Yet you love this marble.

Young walk by,
They have their Nirvana.
They do not notice it.

A squirrel with a leaf
In his mouth selects this one
To make his nest.

The square of marble
Sits on time
Like the mind on meaning.

To be temporal
Is to excite derision
Of marble in winter.

It is so real,
White square,
Is it immortal?

I put my hand on it,
I take it away,
And give it to my love.

Sagacity

What is the use of being sagacious
If wisdom cannot conquer time?
We are sitting at tea in 2500 A.D.
I said love was good
Five hundred years ago.

My times vanished quickly in a mist
But here we are enjoying tea.
We are sitting at tea in 2500 A.D.
Love is still our principle,
Quite dubious, quite good.

If it were not for love we would
Not be begotten but forgotten.
The world is no better and no worse.
You thought of Dante as ancient,
We think of you as prescient.

A Snowfall

As the snow falls I brush it away
With a delicate broom so as not to use a shovel.
Every hour I go out to the long walk,
Conquer the new swirls and pile as if persistence
Were a virtue to keep up with nature.
If I did nothing I would be snowed in.
Some slumberous thinkers think this the best, January.
Let three feet fall, stay indoors, go to sleep,
Luxuriate in sleep like the groundhogs and gray squirrels.

There is something in me to test nature,
To disallow it the archaic predominance,
And if the skies blanket us entirely
With a silence so soft as to be wholly winsome,
(This beguilement of something beyond the human)
I have enough in me to give affront
And take my thin broom against the thick snowflakes
As a schoolmaster who would tell the children
What to do when they are getting sleepy and lazy.

I now make my predicament equal to nature's.
I have the power, although it is timed and limited,
To assert my order against the order of nature.
The snowplows begin to take away the snow,
Flashing big lights in the middle of the night.
They, corporate, have the same idea that I have,
Individualist, not to let nature better us,
But to take this softness and this plenitude
As aesthetic, and control it as it falls.

Trip

If I drive a thousand miles
I feel good.
All those cars none hitting the other.
What a sense of order.

The Capitol in clearest light
In December
Looking small
Beside the Library of Congress.

Who has not loved
To fling himself
Against the New Jersey Turnpike,
Find the Bridge that goes pure North!

Who has not argued the weight
Of national decline,
While not feeling in the least
Supine.

Not crossed the New Jersey Flats
With amusement, wondering
Why, where nothing should jell,
Citizens behave so well.

Nothing but chaos, yet
Reason seems to guide us,
Destinations,
              Destinies.

Wet June

Yellow day-lilies, pressed down by the rain,
Approaching nightfall, lie horizontal touching grass.
It seems unnatural. Will the sun incline them up
Tomorrow? They lie down in complete silence.

Likewise I am pressed down by time toward the end
Of life. I might as well be horizontal in the ground.
My silence is as deep as that of the flowers.

What You Keep
on Your Mantelpiece

Electrical inputs assail our brains
With X-impressions, multifariousness.
We are shocked and doped by immediacy,
Exhilarated and perked by presciences,
Say no, say yes, say whatever,
We are baffled by incommensurables,
Strike back with intellectuality.
We are the new hominids, maculate,
Totally self-sufficient in our destructibility.
Racers of thought, ironists of irony,
Keen on the death of brontosaurus,
Our large basket holding a little wash,
The ideal seems to us ridiculous,
We have killed too many of our enemies
To have any belief in the State,
The sun is going down over the Hudson
Without any idea of right or wrong.
Each of us is touched with heroism
In being alive; the gross jungle
Of the city of ten million breathers
Breathes its essential misunderstanding,
Not knowing what it is to be not knowing.

And I place on the mantelpiece
A picture of the electric spotted cheetah,
Elegant, natural, a killer, to look at.

Coloma

Where Marshall first discovered gold,
By Sutter's Mill in 1849
We paused to think back when
    Millions came to make their way.

With startling rush a great dark buck
Leaped with bounds to take our breath away,
A flash of life amid history.
    Nothing deer can stay.

The Bones of Coleridge

O high hilarity,
O unexpected news,
O English gloom,
Almost Shakespearean,

Certainly Coleridgean,
I am told
By a British lady
Of authority

That the bones
Of Samuel Taylor Coleridge
Could be poked
By boys

Until sixteen years ago.
O high Highgate!
The Highgate folk
Wanted to keep

Him out of Westminster,
Out of local love,
But the churchyard
Grave fell

Into such disrepair
That boys with sticks
Could pester
The bones of Coleridge,

That this was a trick
Boys loved,
To poke a stick
And wiggle the bones of Coleridge,

I say
What a joke,
What youthful expertise
To prize a metaphysician.

The Fort and the Gate

For Machi Razi reading Cavafy

I cannot understand sometimes when I cannot write,
My hand is cold, and my body like a fort
Holds off the attitudes of the world,

As if to say, I am complete, I need not you,
I cannot accept new impressions, but remain
A storehouse full of grains and guns of the past.

I am a fort. I look out at the world
As if I were replete. It is a negative state.
I am stored to repulse any new incursion.

I think life is talking to me thus:
I made you through myriad vicissitudes,
You stand there like eternity.

You are a Platonic Essence, without change.
You stand there in the fort of your being,
Erect, stable, quiet, as if without change.

The barbarians are coming. I open the gate,
And rush out to meet the barbarians.
They are dancing in the sunlight full of life.

I overcome the teachings of my childhood, my parents,
My strong companions who built and fashioned the fort.
I break up the guns of all the people like me.

I rush out and become a barbarian myself.
I rush out and embrace the soul anew.
I die to live, as I live to die.

And now in me there is no eternity
But the reality of the now and new,
I can write out the heart of mankind,

But the people say you have lost your reason,
We must save ourselves, we must kill the barbarians,
But I say, I have learned something beyond you,

I open my gates to the strength of the world,
I embrace the future to become the future,
There is nothing so true and real as change.

From three-foot ancestors, wily-footed and handed,
How long it took to become the Europeans
To make the long march to build Chartres.

What new worlds far hence, what fort, what gate?

A Loon Call

Rowing between Pond and Western Islands
As the tide was coming in
Creating, for so long, two barred islands,
At the end of August, fall nip in the air,
I sensed something beyond me,
Everywhere I felt it in my flesh
As I beheld the sea and sky, the day,
The wordless immanence of the eternal,
And as I was rowing backward
To see directly where I was going,
Harmonious in the freedom of the oars,
A solitary loon cry locked the waters.

Barbaric, indivisible, replete with rack,
Somewhere off where seals were on half-tide rocks,
A loon's cry from beyond the human
Shook my sense to wordlessness.

Perfect cry, ununderstandable essence
Of sound from aeons ago, a shriek,
Strange, palpable, ebullient, wavering,
A cry that I cannot understand,
Praise to the cry that I cannot understand.

Speculative Nature Note

And now as the strength and panorama
Unfolds when evening turns into night,
What should I say of natural splendor,
So foreign to this age?

How could I express the subdued joy
Of waters silent in the long eventide,
How could a poet express
So great a calm, so great a joy?

It is as if all we have suffered,
All we know of temporality,
Were lit with a supernal radiance
Which we cannot believe, but see.

We cannot believe, because of suffering,
But here we see ultimate reality
In a moment of nature, calm, serene,
Before words could speak.

Offering to the Body

I give up to my body the gross fact
That it is not perfect, as I expected
When in youth I preened myself in my excess,
Believing that nothing of it was suspect.

What long day-shine of ramifying revery
I enjoyed in the apple orchard and jungle
Of extreme vegetation when I was replete
With an ardor so powerful it was exact.

Then in those days I loved myself alone,
Was both male and female, both old and young,
Living the long summer days in wholeness, and
In harmony with self and all living beings.

Nothing was so great as to be alive alone
And stand and walk and sit and dream
In the incomparable hours that had no ending,
In endless world of delight that would ever seem.

I offer my body the high estate of my esteem,
I look upon it with joy of its long dream,
I wonder as I wondered when I was young
Of the intricacies and mechanisms of its means.

I am as close to it as to the spiritual,
Although this conglomeration of sinews and muscle
Aggravates time to bring it down to nothing,
Making of the very complex the very simple.

I write to the paradox of the living flesh
That it seems capable but is doomed to end
And while I have a flowing hand may state the truth
That truth is beyond the body, lofted to sky,

So that, seeing the body fail, time take it away,
I offer it the grace of a passing bow of words,
Salute its efforts as its efforts rise and fall,
All a strange tale, and a strange tale to tell.

Survivors

Superior élan
Sometimes offends.
One cannot stand it.
To be clear

In mind and body,
Dominating
A scene at eighty-eight

Makes one think
Too much
On height élan,
Abateless ability,

Breaks reality
Into a special claim
On the nature of man,
Especially of women

Who live longest,
Sometimes an eagle-gilt eye
Surveying the scene
From élan,

Élan's proud claim,
Gives dismay
If humility
Exists,

And if it does not,
Gives dismay
Anyway,
Because

The people suffer,
Have credible
Troubles,
Real heartbreak,

And death comes too soon
To any of them,
These sufferers,
Lauded commoners,

Yet ancient ladies,
Graceful, elegant-pictorial,
Eke on,
Drive from Boston to Maine

At ninety,
Play golf at ninety
At Castine,
A way from sorrow,

It is no ambage
To see these etched beings,
Who have evaded ill
By some mysterious principle

We do not know,
High-spirited,
They spring me
Into empathy

With those who have suffered and lost,
With imperfection,
The common lot,
Nature ruthless,

But the theme of this poem
Is that nature is
Not ruthless to them,
Seemingly,

To have joy at ninety,
Ability to drive a car
Three hundred miles without fatigue
Ought to be celebrated.

I am bemused,
I have seen too much love
Gone wrong,
Lives wasted by time,

Am challenged
By too much
Goddess control,
I cannot accept

That to live long means truth
When I think
Of Keats, of Hopkins,
Of Dylan Thomas.

"I hope to see you next year"
Comes across the bay,
A common report
Carried across the water

On an evening still and full
Of falling sunlight by the ocean.
Of course we do
We all do,

We want five chick swallows
In a nest
Under the areaway
To prosper,

And as the mother and father
Gather bugs
And stuff them
In yellow mouths

We watch the process
Until one day
Five swallows
Take their maiden flight.

They make it
Up to the rooftree,
Sit there expectant,
While mother and father

Fly in to feed them
Still; the next night
They retreat
Near the nest,

Bunched five in a row,
Fed still,
A revelation,
How splendid.

Even after mid July,
The full moon,
The parents feed the young,
Teaching them to fly.

The laws of nature
Are from ancient time,
Why then
Not salute

Old ladies full of grace
Who have
Outwitted time,
Or so it seems,

Continue sportively
Guessing, truthward, at
Genes, environment,
Will, and chance.

The Swinging Bridge

When an hour is harmonious
    Destruction lurks
    Inside the ear.

When you think of good life
    Inside your body
    A wild cell.

When in strength of love
    Imagine the weakness
    To come on you.

What of a thousand years?
    You cannot tout
    The meaning.

Lover to lover, eye to eye,
    Destruction lives, also,
    Inside the eye.

Walk across a swinging bridge,
    Make love in the afternoon.
    That's it. And fit.

Death in a Taxi

Should you die in a bed?
In Rome, under the Pieta,
Bernini's barb in your breast?

Should you die in Alaska,
At Sitka, where the archbishop
Became the Metropolitan of Moscow?

Should you die by the Penobscot,
Two weeks before you did,
Where I reminded you of King Canute

As the tide came up to our chairs
And, while talking, we
Had to move up the beach three times?

Should you die in Ireland,
Foreign to your English ancestry,
For one love, or should you

Die in New York, somewhat foreign
To your Boston background,
For another, the new, or the old?

Should you die in China,
For which you had no affinity,
Or India, too spiritual?

Should you die in a mad house
Where you were often welcome,
The glory of the mind

Announced by Plato, For
The poet is a light and winged
And holy thing, and there is no invention

in him until he has been inspired
And is out of his senses?
You were too sane for this!

Should you die at all?
Do we die at all? No,
Do not die at all,

Cal, but live forever
(We cannot say this)
In your world-managing words.

Should you die in a taxi?
Think of the tradition,
James Agee, Theodore Spencer.

Die in a taxi,
Enroute from one love to another,
Life, love, poetry in transition,

Die in a taxi,
Enroute from one state to another,
The spirit, your spirit, history.

Stone Words
for Robert Lowell

Death, you are so much more powerful
Than all the weepers in all the churches,
Including Boston, that I have
To fight against you with stone words
To put you down, who will not
Be put down, despite man's imagination,
Amplitude, pained intrepidity.

He was your enemy, but couldn't you wait?
He was undefended against you.
You are the mighty one of power.
He and the weepers had to lose,
But let you know, Death,
Poems are slingshot words, Goliath.

In Situ

Self-knowledge is limited expertise.
The crows do not know what they are doing
When they are cawing. A caw god says caw.
They caw, you take it for granted.

If they had better vocal equipment
They might articulate delicate questions,
Enlarge our interest with excitements
To dandle the sound of truth, and articulate
Sensuous gratuities in the orb of the soul.

Man is limited and pulled by strings
Likewise, we take for granted what he says
In Dante and Milton, yet these performances
Disappoint, excite with ultimate lack,
Do not encroach upon the impossible.
If more vocal, he might be able to speak God.

The Play

As a gigantic harp in Vermont
Played in the hills by the air

Lifts and thrills the spirit to see
There in green rondure, a splendid thing,

Waiting for air fingers of sufficient force
For so large an undertaking,

So the spirit makes a music too, of me.

And I am played upon by airy thought
And make an air for you, an air for me,

My shape standing up in the hills
Tall and strange from millions of shoulders,

Man against the sky, man become a harp

Giving off melodious airs in summer time
And venting harmonious tones in winter

Received from heaven and given back

As if man could imagine a harp in the hills
To pluck out of him the delight of his spirit.

Night Thoughts

He shunned the nature of the devil, thinking
I can put you down.
Jealousy, avarice, pain, suspicion
        Flew in his face, and he said
Down, clown, down jester, down savage beast
        You put me down.
I can no longer bear the look of man.
        Everywhere I see
The monster behind the eyeball,
Injustice, cruelty, perversity, spleen,
        An eye of mad anti-heroes
Destroying the earth, fouling the air and waters,
The leer of hatred in blasts of anti-heart
        How do I have the strength
To wrestle with the devil
        When his gleeful power spits in my face?
The wicked, the vain, the treacherous, the sullen
        Thrive high in a world of reason-chill
While the irrationality
        Of my pure source
        Fresh and innocent as childhood's face
        Craves the mighty oracle of the truth,
Creatively I talk
        Of remaking mankind by a breath of love,
        Civilizing and cultivating the elate,
Organizing a better world by care and strength,
        Love the key to put the devil to mischance,
Rise up, holy personages of the salutary heart.

Autumn

Season of bliss and yellow wistfulness,
The corn going down with the sun late afternoon
Haircut of the hills   smokestack of cornfodder
Horses and dogs come down the wood's road.
Thanks for waiting.   Press on the gas.   A white house
Spectacular view of Smarts a postcard mountain
They have painted the old house white to white
Make it new   Bulldozer makes a carpark   black loam
These hills nestle all sorts of hidden life
Old New England   New Old England   Nothing English
Old American.   The Americans have got as old as the hills
Usual talk and then a strange one   makes one strange
More sensitive helpless without trying to help
We do not own the earth   we do not own time
Here it is again   The girl wobbles her face vanishes
Comes back   Something terrible to see and to know
Unconscious three weeks.   Car Crash.   We all go too fast
Now abysmally slow nature tries to bring her back to her.

The Yale Ph.d. candidate is getting it in the neck.
Abysmal depth   No lord of knowledge   He snaps his fingers
At her as if to bring her to   The riches of life now
Depth of suffering   The parents have to take what comes
I do not dare to look into her withdrawn eyes.
Everybody so polite   Nobody discusses the situation
Black drama persuades me to no catharsis.

Think what we think   do what we do   see what we see
We have no hold on fate   the accident of fate
Surrendering to a vast existentialism is called for
The supposition of control is the supposition of life
No control   The brute beast of circumstance blazes on
The uncontrolled hills   the leaves fall one by one
Full of color   Redolent of past dreams   every past mystery
Hopes the harvest   The fields are now shorn   The sun walks
     slowly
Down the valley as stars begin, bitter to choice
Merciless is the reality of the eventide   A cat
Attacks a ball of loam   The mountain broods above
Far off as if to be the more implacable
Mental life has gone on for millennia
Trying to ferret out the meaning of existence
The clap of doom is at the winter door   Snows will
Obstruct society   Not yet   Another gin and tonic
A glass of Scotch   mushrooms savored in sauce   Conversation
Pressing upon the politeness of the year   It is time
To put this house in order but fate will do it to us.

Learning from Nature

While I was
Sitting on the porch, involved in air,
A small bird
Whisked across low,
Four inches from the floor,
Struck a glass door,
A rectangular pane,
With his bill head-on.

He stood dazed
While I looked on amazed,
The silence ponderable.
I wondered
How hurt he was,
Startled
By aerial reality
Piercing contemplation.

Plato was present,
Sophocles, Shakespeare,
Boehme was looking on,
And so was Blake,
Perhaps Dostoevski in a fit
And my friend Angelus Silesius
In the air.
They were interrupted.

The bird suddenly flew
Off into the darkening afternoon.
He did not say how he was.
He was stopped, and he went on.
It taught me acceptance
Of irrationality,
For if he or we could see better
We would know, but we have to go on.